THIS BOOK BELONGS TO:

. . . .

DK | Penguin Random House

Senior Editor James Mitchem
Editor Sally Beets
Design and illustration Victoria Palastanga
Additional design Sadie Thomas
Design assistance Eleanor Bates
Photographer Ruth Jenkinson
Pre-Production Producer Tony Phipps
Senior Producer Inderjit Bhullar
Jacket Co-ordinator Francesca Young
Managing Editor Penny Smith
Managing Art Editor Mabel Chan
Publisher Mary Ling
Art Director Jane Bull

First published in Great Britain in 2018 by
Dorling Kindersley Limited
80 Strand, London, WC2R 0RL

Copyright © 2018 Dorling Kindersley Limited
A Penguin Random House Company
10 9 8 7 6 5 4 3 2 1
001–307865–July/2018

A CIP catalogue record for this book
is available from the British Library.
ISBN: 978-0-2413-1619-1

Printed in China

A WORLD OF IDEAS:
SEE ALL THERE IS TO KNOW

www.dk.com

LET'S MAKE
GREAT
PROJECTS

Contents

Alien invasion

Lion mosaic

Season tree

Shark attack!

Egyptian sarcophagus

ANIMALS

SCIENCE

Grass haircuts

Brilliant bubbles

Let's learn about...
The Solar System

Space is VERY big – bigger than you can possibly imagine! Our planet (Earth) is in a part of space called the Solar System with seven other planets.

Our big neighbour

At the centre of the Solar System is a star called the **Sun**. It's a huge, fiery ball of gas.

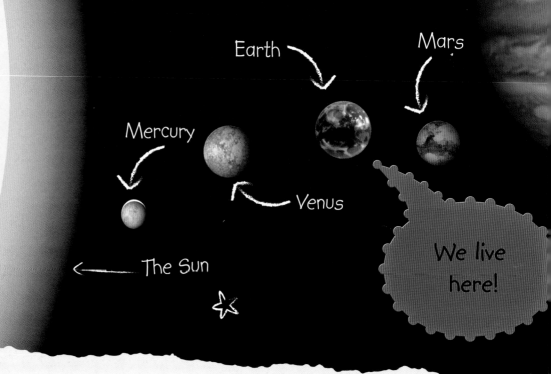

Earth

Mars

Mercury

Venus

The Sun

We live here!

Studying space

It's very difficult to explore space, so scientists use **telescopes** and **probes** to see far away. The probe called Voyager I has travelled beyond the planets!

Saturn

Uranus

Neptune

Jupiter

Make a button Solar System on page 8.

The Solar System is our place in space.

What else is out there?

We don't know! There may be aliens on other planets, but space is really huge and we've only seen a **tiny** part of it so far.

Button **planets**

The real Solar System may be gigantic, but this rotating model of the planets is small enough to twist up and fit in your pocket!

Uranus

Find eight buttons that are similar colours to the planets. Use the biggest one for Jupiter.

Saturn

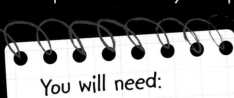

You will need:
- black and yellow card
- scissors
- buttons
- PVA glue
- paintbrush
- split pin

Check the order of the planets on pages 6-7.

① Cut black card into eight strips of different lengths. Cut a yellow circle for the Sun.

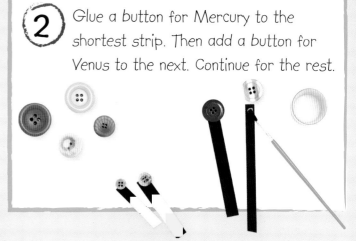

② Glue a button for Mercury to the shortest strip. Then add a button for Venus to the next. Continue for the rest.

Mars

Neptune

Earth is spinning at 1,000 mph (1,600 kph) but because it's a constant speed, we don't notice it.

Mercury is the smallest planet.

Mercury

The Sun

Venus

Jupiter, the biggest planet in the Solar System, has at least 67 moons!

It takes Earth one year to travel around the Sun.

Earth

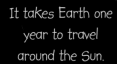

Jupiter

3

Push a split pin through the Sun and the end of each black strip.

The buttons can move around the Sun – just like in the real Solar System.

Marshmallow constellations

If you look at the night sky you might spot a bear, a hunter, or a flying horse as patterns in the stars. Make your own that you can eat.

You will need:
- white pencil
- black paper
- toothpicks
- marshmallows

1 Map out your chosen star constellation on a piece of black paper.

2 Join the toothpicks and marshmallows together and place on top to create the constellation.

You may need to snap the toothpicks to make them shorter.

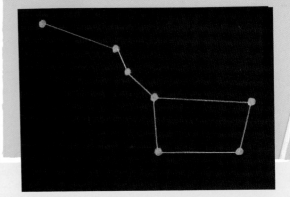

Stars look tiny because they are really far away. Most are much bigger than Earth!

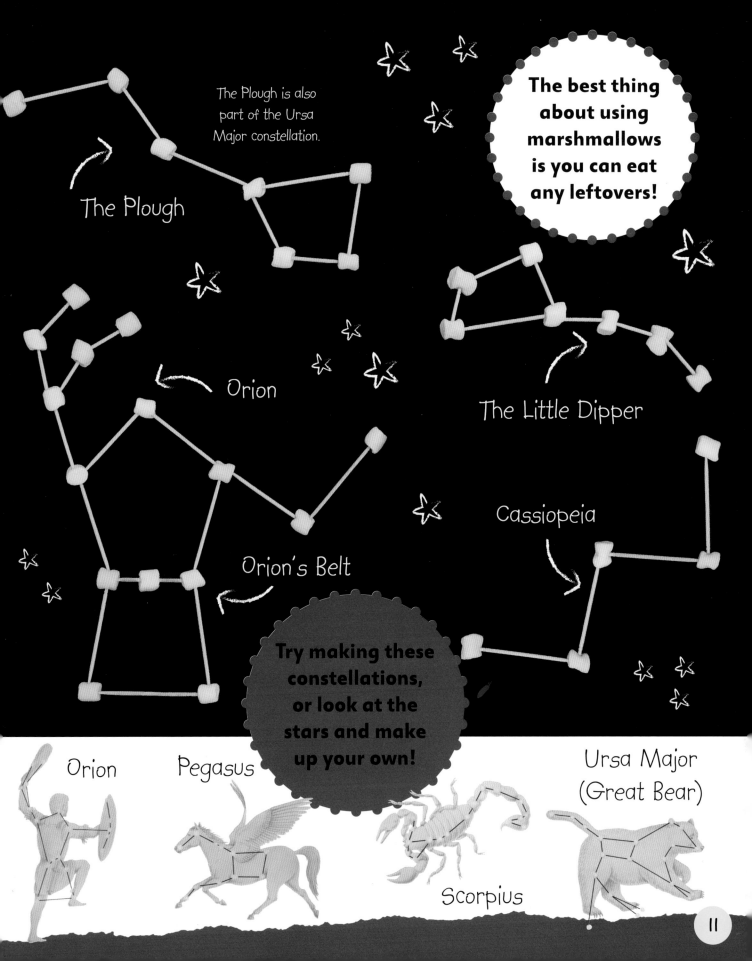

The Plough

The Plough is also part of the Ursa Major constellation.

The best thing about using marshmallows is you can eat any leftovers!

Orion

The Little Dipper

Cassiopeia

Orion's Belt

Try making these constellations, or look at the stars and make up your own!

Orion

Pegasus

Scorpius

Ursa Major (Great Bear)

Alien **invasion**

Could there be strange alien beings living on planets far away? Nobody knows, but it's fun to make potato prints of what they might look like!

You will need:
- potato
- knife
- paint
- paper
- paintbrushes
- googly eyes

Carefully slice a potato in half. Dip the flat side into paint and then print it onto paper. Paint on arms, legs, and other features, then add googly eyes to finish the aliens.

Use bright colours for your aliens.

Let's learn about...
Space travel

People have always wondered what it's like among the stars, but getting to space is hard. However, thanks to clever scientists and technology, we know more about space travel than ever.

Rocket

Learn to make straw rockets on page 16.

Living in space
Astronauts use rockets to launch them into space. While they're in space, many astronauts live and work at the **International Space Station**.

One small step for man, one giant leap for mankind.

Amazing astronauts

The people who travel to space are called astronauts. Their special space suits help them breathe and survive the harsh conditions of space.

Satellite

Space suit

International Space Station

Make your own space outfit on pages 20-23.

The Moon Landing

In 1969 astronauts landed on the Moon, but so far nobody has visited another planet.

15

Straw **rockets**

Rockets help astronauts travel to outer space. These ones won't make it quite that far, but they will fly across the room! Three, two, one, LIFT OFF!

You will need:
- colouring pencils
- paper
- scissors
- wide straw
- thin tape
- thin straw

The Saturn V rocket helped astronauts reach the Moon for the first time. The journey took three days.

1 Draw pictures of rockets onto paper and cut them out.

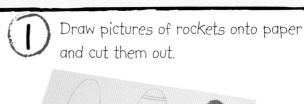

2 Snip off a section of the wide straw that is almost as long as the rocket. Squeeze the end and tape it shut.

3 Tape the wide straw to the back of the rocket as shown. Fit a thinner straw inside it.

Scientists hope to build a rocket that can travel to Mars. It would be the most powerful rocket ever!

Take your rocket outside and see how far it glides. Use chalk to mark the distance on the ground.

Blow into the end of the straw and watch the rocket fly away!

whoosh!

zoooom!

We have LIFT OFF!

17

Space patches

Every space mission has its own special patch made for the crew. If you want to be like a real astronaut, you'll need one, too.

You will need:
- pencil
- card
- scissors
- coloured felt
- ruler
- PVA glue
- paintbrush
- tape
- safety pin

Real patches from various NASA missions:

Apollo 7

Apollo 8

Apollo 16

Gemini 6

Gemini 9

Gemini 12

Many patches include the names of the astronauts.

The American space agency, NASA, stands for "National Aeronautics and Space Administration".

Space patches often feature pictures related to the mission's goal.

1 Draw and cut out a large and small circle on card. Trace the templates onto felt and cut them out.

②

Draw pieces of a rocket on card and cut them out to use as a template.

③

Place the templates onto felt and trace around them. Cut out the shapes and glue them together. Leave to dry.

④

Glue the back of the patch to the large card circle and tape on a safety pin.

Try these designs, or invent your own!

Pin your patches to your clothes to really show them off!

Bottle **jetpack**

There isn't much gravity out in space, so astronauts use jetpacks to stop them from floating away. Make this one and you'll be ready to zoom!

You will need:

- pen
- cardboard
- scissors
- red foam
- PVA glue
- paintbrush
- strong tape
- two large plastic bottles
- foil
- cream card
- felt
- coloured tape
- bottle tops

1 Draw and cut out a cardboard base using the template on page 78.

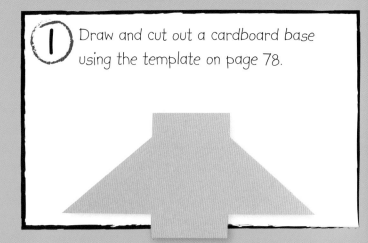

2 Cut four foam triangles for the wings and glue them to both sides of the cardboard.

Make sure the straps are long enough to fit your arms through.

3 Fold two long pieces of tape back on themselves to make straps. Tape at the top and bottom to hold in place.

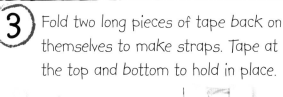

4

Cover the bottles in foil and tape them together. Wrap cream card around the bottles and tape to secure.

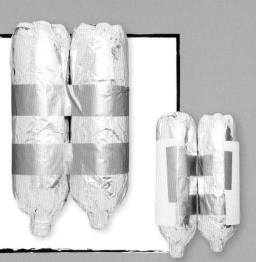

Decorate your jetpack with coloured tape and bottle tops.

5

Tape around the top and bottom of the bottles, looping it through the straps.

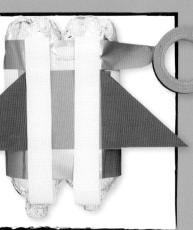

6

Draw and cut out fire shapes from felt and tape them to the neck of each bottle.

Jetpacks release bursts of gas. The force created by this propels the astronaut in the opposite direction.

Space **helmet**

Astronauts wear space suits with helmets when they're in outer space. They wouldn't be able to survive the harsh conditions without them!

You will need:
- 1 cup PVA glue
- 1 cup flour
- 1 cup water
- newspaper
- blown-up balloon
- cup
- scissors
- blue and white paint
- paintbrush

Helmets protect against the intense pressure of space. Real helmets are also linked to oxygen tanks so the astronaut can breathe.

① Combine the glue, flour, and water. Dip strips of newspaper in the mix and cover the balloon with at least three layers.

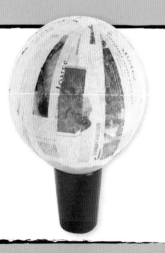

② Leave to dry. Once it's fully set, pop the balloon and remove it from the inside of the paper.

③ Trim the bottom of the shape to fit your head through. Paint the inside blue, and the outside white.

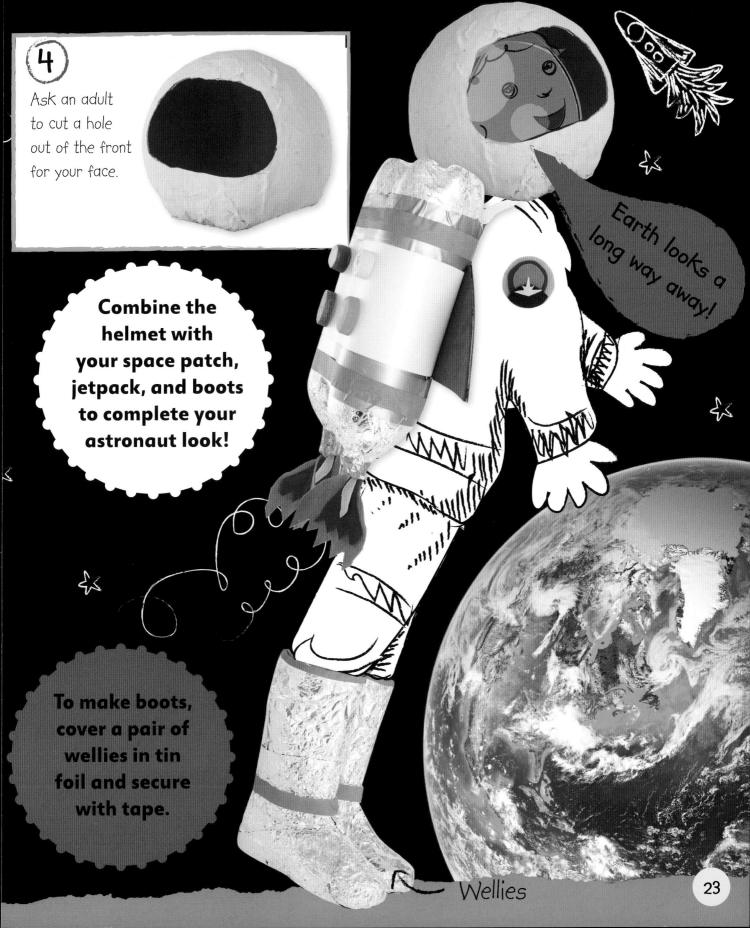

4 Ask an adult to cut a hole out of the front for your face.

Combine the helmet with your space patch, jetpack, and boots to complete your astronaut look!

Earth looks a long way away!

To make boots, cover a pair of wellies in tin foil and secure with tape.

Wellies

Let's learn about...
The seasons

Much of the world has four seasons. Plants, animals, weather, and the amount of daylight are all affected as the seasons change.

Birds build nests.

Leaves sprout.

Flowers blossom.

The weather in **spring** is unpredictable. It can be sunny and rainy. It's during spring that most plants start to bloom.

Birds sing more often.

Summer has the longest days, and is usually warm, sunny, and dry.

What causes the seasons to change?

The Earth is **tilted**. So as the Earth moves around the Sun, different parts of the world tilt toward or away from it at different times of year.

Turn the page to make a season tree model.

Make a special nature mask on page 30.

Leaves change colour and fall.

Many trees are bare.

I'm collecting food for winter.

In **autumn** the weather starts to grow colder.

Snow can fall.

Winter has short days with less sunlight, and is usually cold.

Some animals sleep through winter.

Four or two?
Not everywhere on Earth has the same seasons. Tropical countries are hot all year round, but have a **wet** and **dry** season.

Season **tree**

Have you noticed that some trees look different throughout the year? Capture the beauty of all four seasons with this model tree.

You will need:
- pencil
- round plate
- card
- orange, green, pink, blue, and brown sheets of card
- PVA glue
- paint
- paintbrushes
- paper
- things to decorate with, such as pom-poms and glitter

① Draw an outline of a tree onto card, using a plate for the circle. Cut it out.

② Draw around the card template onto sheets of orange, green, pink, and blue card. Cut these out.

③ Sketch the outline of a tree trunk and branches onto the template and cut it out.

4

On brown card, draw around the trunk template and cut out a trunk. Repeat three times, so you have four trunks.

5 Glue the trunks onto each coloured tree as pictured.

Some parts of the world only have two seasons; one rainy and one dry.

6

Paint different colours onto paper. Once dry, cut out lots of leaf and grass shapes to decorate with.

Mix the colours to create lots of pretty shades.

Blossom

Berries

Snow

Spring

Summer

Autumn

Winter

Pom-poms, glitter, cotton wool, or foam will make your season tree look extra special.

⑦ Glue the leaves and grass, along with pom-poms, glitter, and any other decorations to each tree. Make each look like a season.

⑧ In season order (spring, summer, autumn, winter), gently fold each tree inward down the centre, and then glue the back of one half to half of the next tree.

Nature **mask**

The natural world is a treasure trove of beautiful materials. Go on a nature hunt and see what you discover, then use your finds to create a mask!

You will need:

- scissors
- black or cream card
- pen
- sticky tack
- elastic
- PVA glue
- paintbrush
- leaves and natural items

Many trees shed their leaves during autumn and winter, but "evergreen" trees keep their leaves all year round.

① Cut a mask shape from card. Ask an adult to help cut eye holes.

② Push a pen through each side of the card into a piece of sticky tack to make holes. Thread the elastic through the holes and fasten.

③ Glue your leaves and other items onto the mask.

Look out for other natural treasures such as seeds, feathers, and flowers to decorate your mask.

You can find beautiful coloured leaves in autumn.

Only use items you find on the ground.

Let's learn about...
Weather

Hot or cold, wet or dry, snowy or sunny – weather is the name for what is happening in the air around us.

Rain falls from clouds. It gets us wet but gives us water to drink and helps plants grow.

Sun warms up our world and is responsible for how hot we feel. This is called temperature.

Meteorologist

Meteorologists use weather symbols.

Tell the time with a sundial on page 34.

Weather reporters

People who study the weather are called "meteorologists". They use special machines to predict and record the weather.

Weather warning!

Extreme weather can have dramatic effects. Storms cause floods and damage to buildings, and too much hot weather can cause fires and kill crops.

Snow falls from clouds when it's very cold. It eventually melts into water.

Wind is air that is moving around. Use the wind's power to make chimes on page 38.

What causes weather?

The Sun heats up some parts of the world more than others. These differences in temperature create winds that move clouds around.

Wind turbine

Powered by the weather

Clever inventions like solar panels and wind turbines turn energy from weather into electricity.

Smiling **sundial**

Did you know you can use the Sun to tell the time? All you need is a sunny day, something to cast a shadow, and a little bit of patience!

You will need:
- yellow paint
- paintbrush
- paper plate
- scissors
- pen
- straw
- sticky tack

Save this project for the summer when there are lots of sunny days.

① Paint the plate yellow.

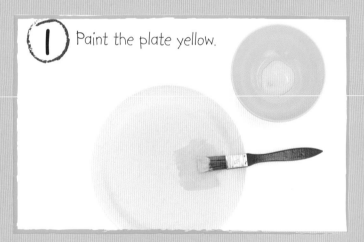

② Snip 12 triangles evenly round the outside of the plate. Use a pen to poke a hole through the middle.

③ Draw a smiley face and put a straw through the hole.

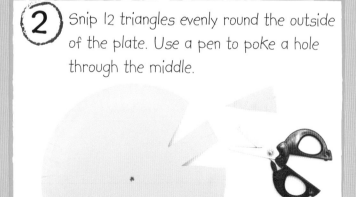

What's the time?

The sun is at its highest point in the sky at midday.

Earth rotates once a day, making it look like the Sun moves across the sky. As the Sun changes position, the shadows it casts move too.

To use your sundial, go outside at midday and line up the shadow made by the straw with the top of your sundial. Write "12" there.

Every hour, write the next number in line with where the shadow has moved to.

Stick your sundial down with sticky tack so it doesn't move or blow away.

Measure **the rain**

Ever wondered how much rain falls in a day? With your own rain gauge, you can take part in an experiment to find out!

You will need:
- scissors
- plastic bottle
- marker pens
- ruler
- stones
- water

Plants needs water to survive, so rain is very important.

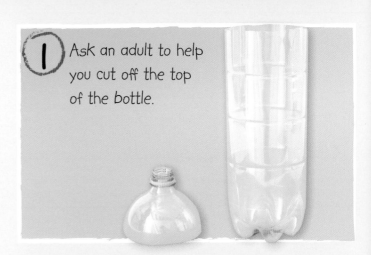

1. Ask an adult to help you cut off the top of the bottle.

2. Draw a ring around the bottle near the bottom. Mark measurements above it with a ruler and marker pens.

3. Fill the bottle with stones up to your ring and cover with water. Slot the upside-down top of the bottle inside.

Stones

The top of the bottle flipped upside-down acts as a funnel.

Use permanent markers to decorate the bottle, so the rain doesn't wash it away!

The stones will help stop your bottle from falling over.

What causes rain?

When water is warmed by the Sun, it turns into invisible water vapour and rises upward. This is called "evaporation".

When the vapour cools it "condenses". This means it turns into water droplets and forms clouds. When the droplets get big enough they fall as rain.

Make a chart like this and record how much rain falls over several days.

	Day 1	Day 2	Day 3	D
Rainfall (cm/in)				

37

Wind **chimes**

Don't throw away your old baked bean tins! Turn them into pretty wind chimes and listen to them jingle-jangle in the garden.

You will need:
- tins
- coloured tape
- coloured elastic bands
- hammer
- screw or nail
- wool
- pom-poms
- needle
- branch

Your wind chimes will make beautiful, relaxing sounds when they blow in the breeze.

Tape around the rim of the tin – it will be sharp.

Decorate tins by wrapping coloured tape and elastic bands around them.

Ask an adult to make a hole in the bottom of the tin by tapping it with a hammer and screw.

Hole

Try attaching spoons, keys, or other items to your wind chimes and see if the sounds change.

The pom-poms make your wind chimes look pretty.

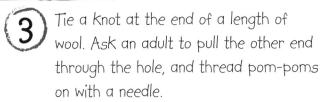

③ Tie a knot at the end of a length of wool. Ask an adult to pull the other end through the hole, and thread pom-poms on with a needle.

Knot

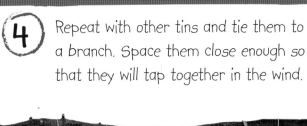

④ Repeat with other tins and tie them to a branch. Space them close enough so that they will tap together in the wind.

Let's learn about...
Ancient Egypt

The Ancient Egyptians ruled for more than 3,000 years. They are famous for their amazing pyramids, their many gods, and their strong rulers.

Pyramid →

I'm in charge!

Egyptians grew wheat.

Pharaoh

Who was in charge?
Powerful kings and queens called **pharaohs** ruled Ancient Egypt. They were thought of and treated like they were living gods.

The mighty Nile
The River Nile – the longest in the world – was important to the Egyptians because the soil left behind after it flooded was great for growing **crops**.

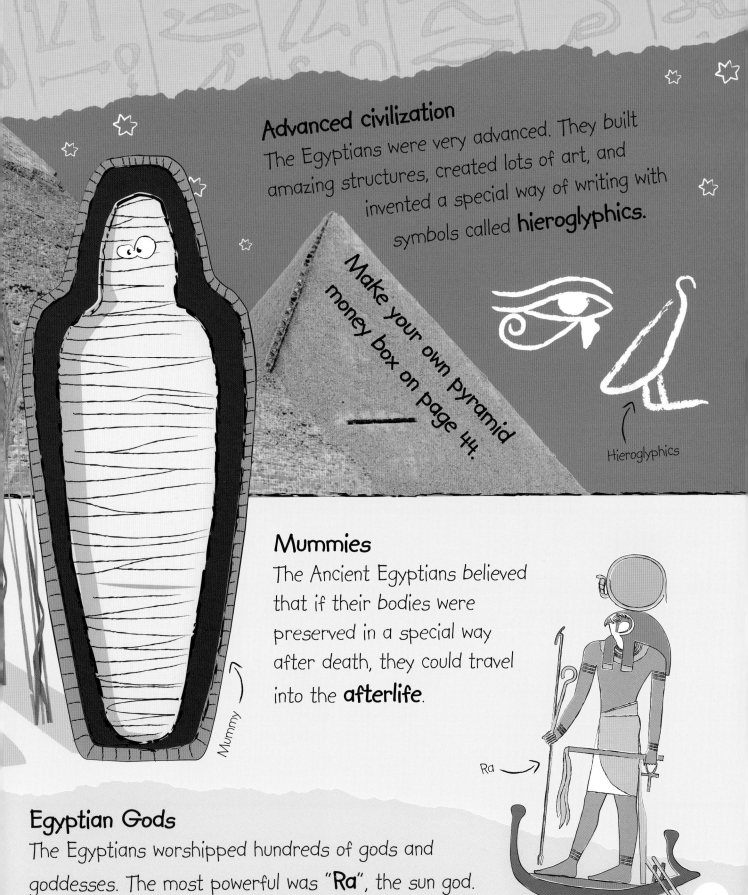

Advanced civilization

The Egyptians were very advanced. They built amazing structures, created lots of art, and invented a special way of writing with symbols called **hieroglyphics.**

Make your own Pyramid money box on page 44.

Hieroglyphics

Mummies

The Ancient Egyptians believed that if their bodies were preserved in a special way after death, they could travel into the **afterlife**.

Mummy

Ra

Egyptian Gods

The Egyptians worshipped hundreds of gods and goddesses. The most powerful was "**Ra**", the sun god.

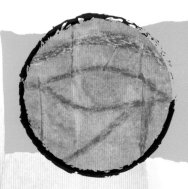

Papyrus **scroll**

The Ancient Egyptians used special symbols as writing. These "hieroglyphics" were written on something called papyrus.

You will need:
- brown paper bag
- PVA glue
- paintbrush
- tea towel
- crayons

Paper didn't exist when the Egyptians lived. They crushed up papyrus leaves and weaved them together to write on.

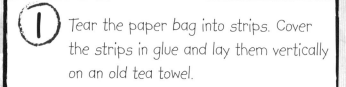

① Tear the paper bag into strips. Cover the strips in glue and lay them vertically on an old tea towel.

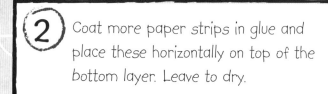

② Coat more paper strips in glue and place these horizontally on top of the bottom layer. Leave to dry.

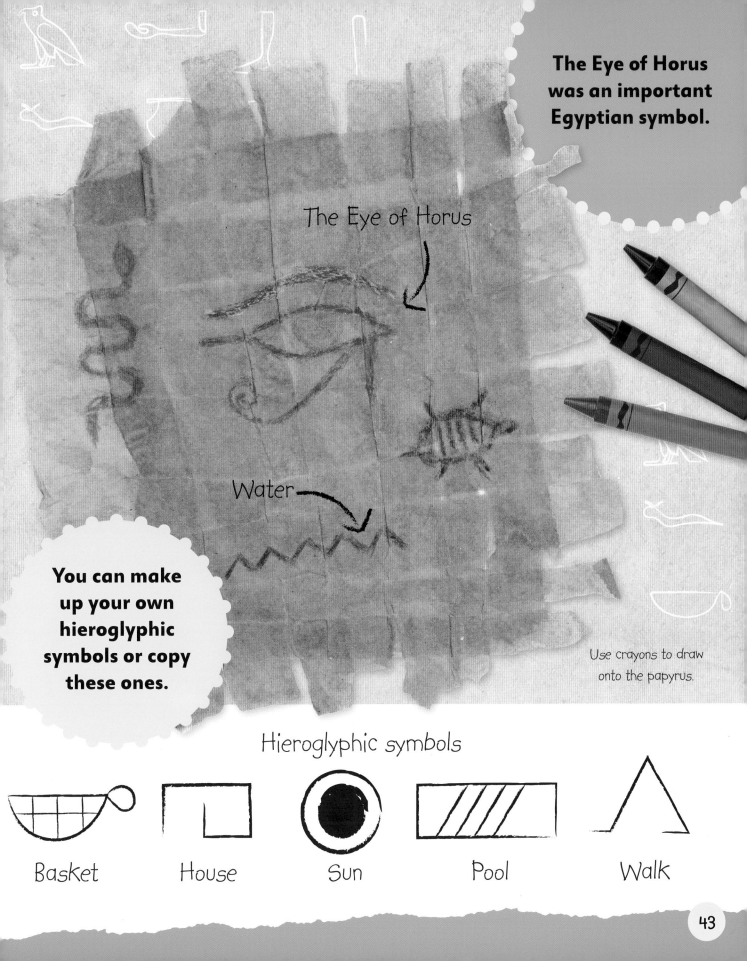

The Eye of Horus
was an important
Egyptian symbol.

The Eye of Horus

Water

You can make
up your own
hieroglyphic
symbols or copy
these ones.

Use crayons to draw
onto the papyrus.

Hieroglyphic symbols

Basket   House   Sun   Pool   Walk

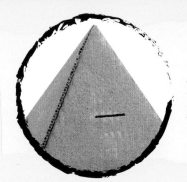

Pyramid **money box**

Egyptian pharoahs expected to live forever as gods. They built huge pyramids to be buried in with their treasure.

You will need:

- ruler
- cardboard
- pencil
- scissors
- circular lid
- PVA glue
- paintbrush
- sand

Fill your money box with coins, so it's like the treasure in a real pyramid!

1 Measure and cut out the template on page 79. Make sure to include the tabs, and cut a thin slot into one of the triangles.

Tab

Slot

2 Draw around the lid in the middle of the square base. Cut this out, then snip all the way into the edge of the circle.

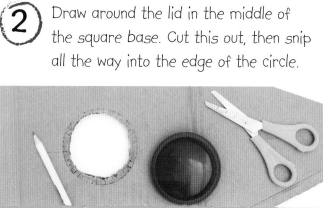

3 Fold the sides up and glue the outside of each tab to attach it to the triangle next to it.

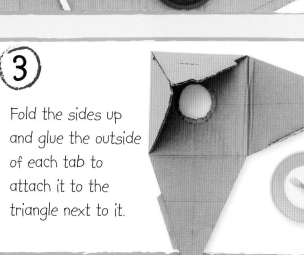

4 Combine glue with sand and use it to cover your pyramid.

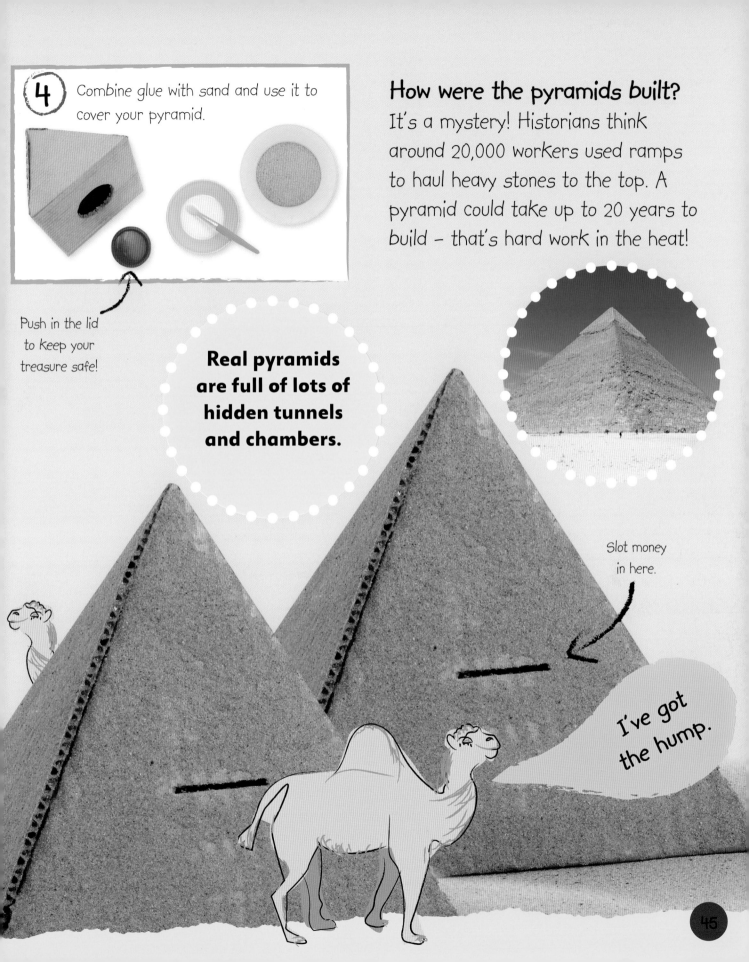

Push in the lid to keep your treasure safe!

How were the pyramids built?
It's a mystery! Historians think around 20,000 workers used ramps to haul heavy stones to the top. A pyramid could take up to 20 years to build – that's hard work in the heat!

Real pyramids are full of lots of hidden tunnels and chambers.

Slot money in here.

I've got the hump.

Egyptian **sarcophagus**

When very important people in Ancient Egypt died, they were wrapped in bandages and placed in a sarcophagus (a special coffin) for the afterlife.

You will need:

- doll
- bandages
- black paper
- 1 long and 1 short crisp tube
- scissors
- tape
- pencil
- white card
- felt-tip pens
- double-sided tape

This burial process is called mummification.

1 Turn your doll into a mummy by wrapping it from head to toe in bandages.

2 Make a design for the body and head on card. Do them separately and make sure they fit the tubes.

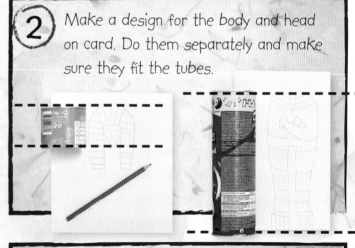

3 Cover both tubes with black paper and cut to size. Secure with tape.

4 Colour your designs and stick them onto the tubes with double-sided tape.

Slide your mummy into its sarcophagus and put the top on.

Bury me with my favourite accessories!

Making a mummy

Only pharaohs and the very wealthy could afford to be made into mummies. The process was long, complicated, and VERY gruesome. Here's how it worked:

• The brain was removed through the nose with a special hook.

• Other organs were removed by people called "embalmers".

• The body was dried out using a salty mixture.

• The body was wrapped in linen and placed in the sarcophagus for the afterlife.

Mummies were buried with their belongings so they could take them into the afterlife.

Let's learn about...
The Roman Empire

At the height of its power, the Roman Empire spanned three continents. More than 60 million people lived there, making it one of the strongest empires in history. But what made the Romans so successful?

Make your own shield on page 50.

This "tortoise formation" kept soldiers well protected.

A very strong army
Nobody could match the might of the Romans. Their army of warriors (legionaries) was huge, and they used clever tactics to defeat their enemies.

Create a lion mosaic on page 54.

Roman coins

I came, I saw, I conquered!

Roman emperor

We're wonderful!

They were cultured

Many Roman citizens wore clothing made from fine fabric. They also loved art, theatre, and entertainment.

Happy citizens are much easier to rule than unhappy ones!

The Colosseum

Talent for building

The Romans were master **builders**. They built cities, bridges, waterways, and lots of roads that helped them spread across the world.

49

Roman **shield**

Roman soldiers defended themselves with strong shields made of wood and metal. This is how to make one big enough to cover your whole body.

You will need:

- pen
- cardboard
- scissors
- red paint
- paintbrush
- gold paper
- silver paint
- PVA glue
- strong tape

Many shields were red, the colour of Mars, the Roman god of war.

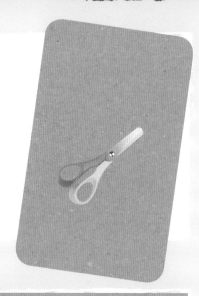

Draw a large rectangle onto cardboard and cut it out. Round off the corners.

Cover one side in red paint and slightly bend the edges so that the shield curves inward.

③ Draw decorative designs (or copy these) onto gold paper and cut them out.

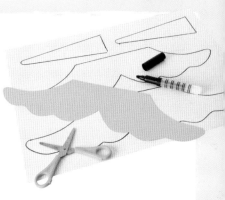

4 Cut a cardboard square and circle for a "boss". Paint these silver and glue them and the decorations to the front.

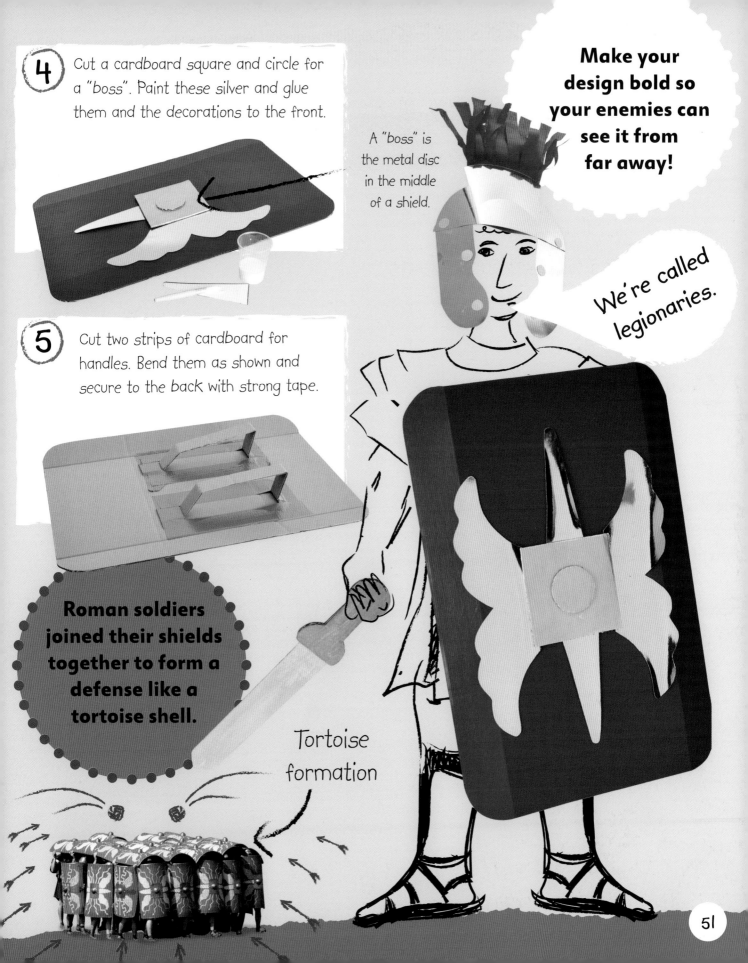

A "boss" is the metal disc in the middle of a shield.

Make your design bold so your enemies can see it from far away!

We're called legionaries.

5 Cut two strips of cardboard for handles. Bend them as shown and secure to the back with strong tape.

Roman soldiers joined their shields together to form a defense like a tortoise shell.

Tortoise formation

Cookie **coins**

The Roman Empire was very wealthy, so they had to have a lot of special coins. You can't spend these ones, but you can eat them – which is much better!

You will need:
- cookies (either shop bought or homemade)
- writing icing

Make your own cookies

Preheat the oven to 180°C (350°F/Gas 4) and line a baking sheet with baking paper.

Combine 100g (3½oz) butter with 125g (4½oz) sugar with an electric whisk. Beat in an egg and ½ tsp vanilla extract. Then stir in 150g (5½oz) self-raising flour.

Roll into 18 balls and place on a baking sheet. Flatten and cook for 12-15 minutes.

1. Bake your cookies (if using homemade).

2. Use writing icing to add decoration.

Numbers	1	2	3	4	5	6	7	8	9	10
Roman numerals	I	II	III	IV	V	VI	VII	VIII	IX	X

Roman numerals

The Roman number system used different combinations of letters. Numbers placed before or after each other were either added or subtracted. So 5 (V) + 1 (I) = 6 (VI).

Add faces or numerals to your cookies.

Can you work out your age in Roman numerals? Why not put it on a cookie?

Romans often put the faces of their emperors on their coins.

Lion **mosaic**

Romans decorated the floors of their buildings with mosaics, which were pictures made up of lots of tiny pieces of stone. Let's make a paper version!

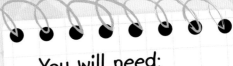

You will need:
- coloured paper
- scissors
- pencil
- glue stick

Mosaics often showed scenes from history, animals, or daily life. Copy this lion, or create your own design.

1 Cut paper into strips.

2 Snip the strips horizontally to make tiny squares.

3 Draw a pencil outline of your design on paper and glue on the squares.

Add a border.

Having a fancy mosaic in your home was a sign that you were rich!

Romans were fascinated by exotic animals such as lions. Crowds would watch gladiators fight lions at the Colosseum.

Let's learn about...
The animal kingdom

Our world is full of animals, from giant giraffes roaming the plains, to tiny insects burrowing underground. We split the world's animals into six main groups.

I'm the fastest land animal.

Dragonfly

Beetle

Spider

Snail

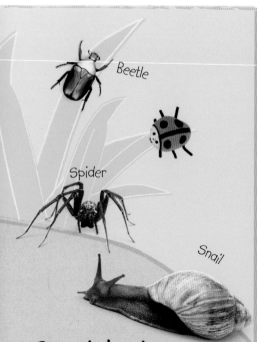

Cheetah

Fish
These animals live in fresh or salt water. They breathe through slits in their sides called gills.

Angelfish

Shark

Mammals
Mammals are warm-blooded and feed their young with milk. Most have fur and teeth.

Giraffe

Turn cardboard into wild animals on page 64

Invertebrates
There are more animals in this group than any other. One thing they have in common is they don't have backbones in their bodies.

Chimpanzee

Paint stone birds on page 58.

Did you know that people are mammals?

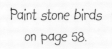

Parrot

Crocodile

Amphibians

These animals are born in water with gills and tails, but move to land when they get bigger and grow legs.

Reptiles

Reptiles have scaly skin and are cold-blooded. This means they can't get warm without the Sun.

Birds

These feathered animals have wings, but not all of them can fly!

Penguin

Tadpole

Frog

There are thousands of different animals, but all of them need to eat and breathe.

Snake

Stone **creatures**

From cats, to owls, to creepy-crawlies, you can find amazing animals right on your doorstep. But if you make your own they'll always be nearby.

You will need:
- paint
- paintbrushes
- stones
- fine-liner pen
- scissors
- felt
- PVA glue

1 To make an owl, paint most of a stone brown, leaving space for a face and body.

2 Once this has dried, use a thin brush and fine-liner pen to add detail.

3 Finish your owl by cutting feet and a beak from felt and gluing them on.

Once you've made an owl, why not try these other creatures too?

Bugs like to hide in dark, damp places...

You can't catch me, Wormy!

Use a magnifying glass to get a closer look at bugs.

Keep a list of any animals that you spot in the wild.

Remember that most wild animals like to be left alone.

59

Bird **feeder**

Hang a bird feeder in your garden so that birds can flock there for food. It's the perfect way to learn about the birds that live in your local area.

The best time to hang a feeder is in autumn, when birds are preparing for winter.

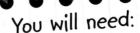

Tweet! Tweet!

You will need:

- 2 packs gelatine powder
- 400ml (14fl oz) boiling water
- bowl
- 200g (9oz) birdseed
- cookie cutters
- tray
- straws
- scissors
- ribbon

Ask an adult to dissolve the gelatine in the water. Then stir in the birdseed.

Lay cookie cutters on a tray, fill with the mix, and push a straw through each one. Leave in the fridge to set overnight.

You can tie on a cookie cutter to fit around your feeder. It frames it beautifully.

Birds are most active in the morning, so that's the best time to watch your feeder.

Glue on a stick to give the birds a place to perch.

③ Once the shapes have set, remove the cookie cutters. Trim the straws, then thread ribbon through the holes.

④ Secure the ribbon in place with a knot.

Making **tracks**

Trot, waddle, or stride? The tracks left by animals give us clues about their behaviour. Try leaving some footprints of your own.

You will need:
- pen
- paper
- scissors
- firm sponges
- PVA glue
- flip flops
- paint
- paintbrushes

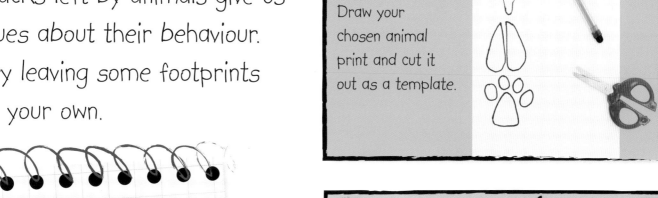

1 Draw your chosen animal print and cut it out as a template.

2 Place the templates onto sponges. Draw around them and cut them out.

Chicken

Dog

Deer

③ Glue the sponges to the bottom of your flip flops and leave to set.

④ Paint the sponge and go for a walk, but only where you won't make a mess!

Real animal tracks show up in mud or snow. Keep an eye out for them.

Only walk on paper or cardboard so you don't get paint everywhere!

Red deer prints

Copy my tracks if you're not too chicken!

Cardboard **giraffe**

Long necks, scales, stripes, and tails... animals come in all shapes and sizes. Have a go at making your own.

You will need:
- scissors
- long cardboard tubes
- paints
- paintbrush
- card
- pen
- PVA glue

The place where an animal lives is called a "habitat".

① Cut a cardboard tube in half widthwise. Then cut one of the halves lengthwise into four strips.

② Fold the strips in half vertically. Paint the pieces to look like the legs and body of a giraffe.

③ Carefully cut thin holes into the bottom of the tube and slide the legs into them.

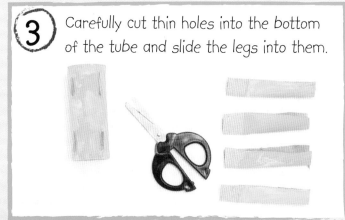

4 Draw the outline of a giraffe's head and tail as shown. Paint them, then cut them out.

5 Cut a hole in the cardboard tube for the neck to slot into, then glue on the tail.

Many animals have special features that make them well suited to their habitats.

Hissss! I'm camouflaged.

Stripes make zebras hard to spot in long grass.

Monkeys' tails help them hang from trees.

Long necks help giraffes eat from tall trees.

Why not make the giraffe some friends?

65

Shark **attack!**

Some animals only eat plants, but others hunt and eat other animals. Sharks are some of the best hunters in the world. Make this shark's jaws move!

 1

Draw and cut out an outline of a shark head, a little fish, and six long strips.

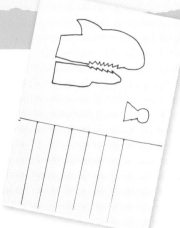

You will need:

- pen
- card
- scissors
- paintbrush
- paint
- pin
- split pins
- googly eyes

 **2**

Paint the strips and shark grey, but don't paint the teeth. Use another colour for the little fish.

3 Make three crosses with the strips and push a split pin through each one.

Press a pin into the card to make a hole, then insert the split pin and pull apart to secure.

4 Insert four more split pins as shown, then use two more to attach the shark's head and jaws.

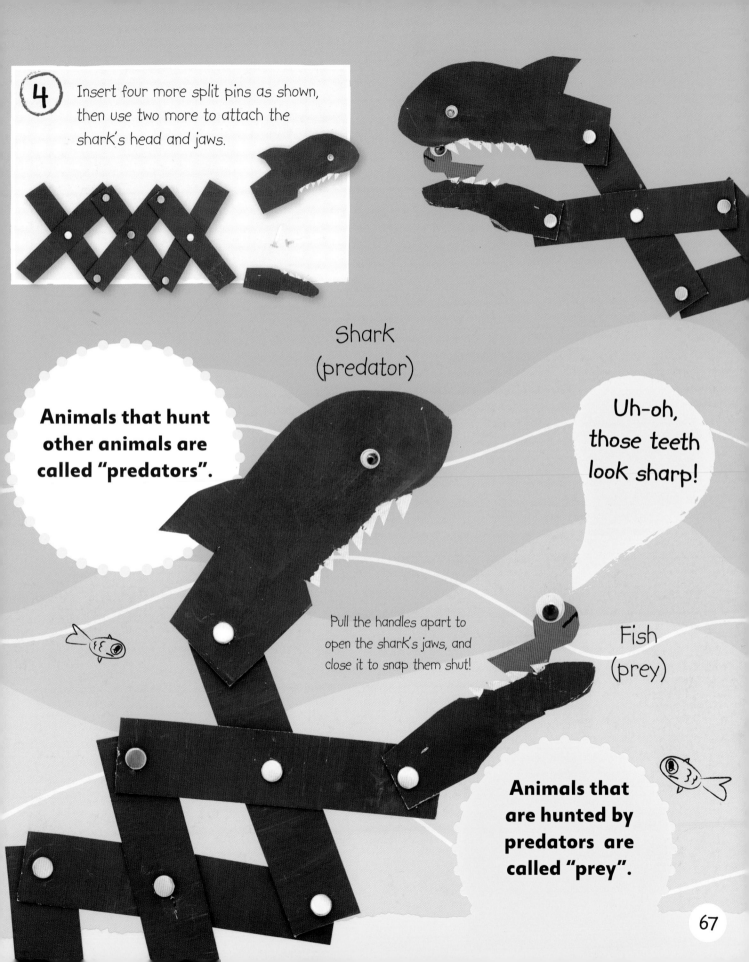

Shark
(predator)

Animals that hunt other animals are called "predators".

Uh-oh, those teeth look sharp!

Pull the handles apart to open the shark's jaws, and close it to snap them shut!

Fish
(prey)

Animals that are hunted by predators are called "prey".

Let's learn about...
Science

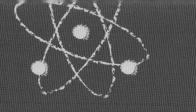

Science doesn't just take place in labs – it's happening all around us all the time! Science is the study of the Universe, everything in it, and how it all works.

Science is split into three main groups: physics, chemistry, and biology.

Make brilliant bubbles on page 72.

Anything involving light, sound, forces, and energy belongs to the group called **physics**.

Super scientists
The people who study science are called scientists. It's their job to ask questions and do experiments.

Find out why I need a haircut on page 70.

See a real chemical reaction on page 76.

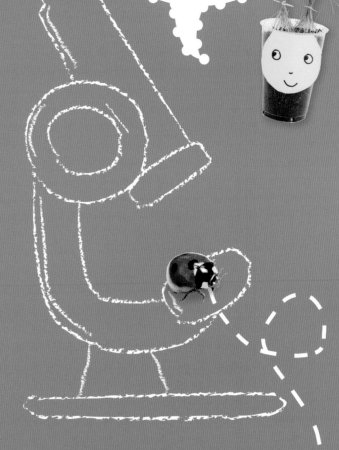

Science that examines what things are made of is called **chemistry**.

The study of living things and how they work – including you – is **biology**.

Thanks, science!

Everything from creating new technology and curing diseases, to launching rockets into space, is possible because of science.

Grass **haircuts**

Plants are living things that need taking care of to survive. If you look after your grass plant well, it will grow enough to need a trim!

You will need:
- soil
- grass seeds
- plastic cups
- water

Plants need air, light, and water to grow. Experiment by keeping one plant in a dark place to see if it grows differently.

1

Plant grass seeds in soil and water once a day.

2

Keep your plants in a sunny spot and check in daily to see how much they grow.

Draw on faces or use a photo of yourself.

Measure how much the grass grows each day and write it down.

Ah! That's better – a nice haircut.

You can plant seeds in egg shells.

Give the grass a haircut!

About time!

71

Brilliant **bubbles**

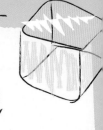

Bubbles are usually round, but it is possible to create square and pyramid bubbles in 3D frames using a little science!

You will need:
- 4 cups water
- ½ cup washing-up liquid
- 4 tbsp glycerine
- bowl
- pipe cleaners
- scissors

The glycerine will make your bubbles super strong.

1 To make your bubble solution, mix together water, washing up liquid, and glycerine. Leave overnight.

2 Cut and bend three pipe cleaners as shown, then join them all together.

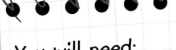

3 Attach two shorter pipe cleaner pieces and shape them into a cube, as shown.

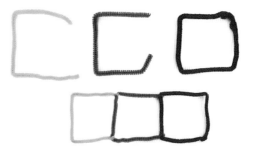

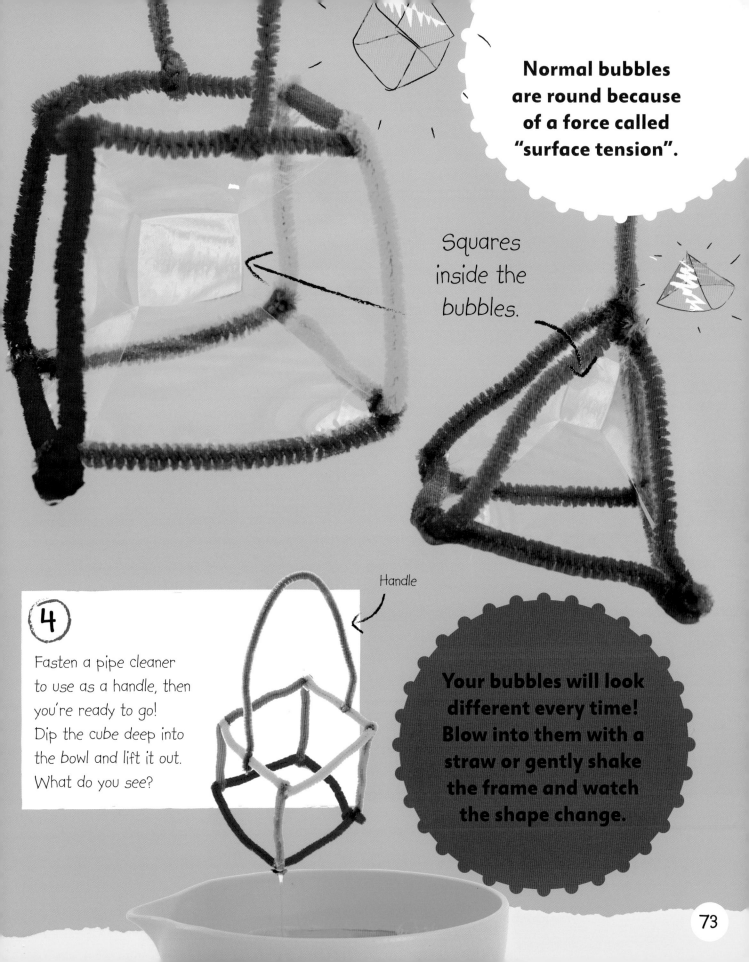

Normal bubbles are round because of a force called "surface tension".

Squares inside the bubbles.

Handle

Your bubbles will look different every time! Blow into them with a straw or gently shake the frame and watch the shape change.

(4)

Fasten a pipe cleaner to use as a handle, then you're ready to go! Dip the cube deep into the bowl and lift it out. What do you see?

Liquid **layers**

Did you know you can stack liquids on top of each other? It might look like magic, but it's because of something called "density". Let's put it to the test!

① Pour honey into the glass. Add the other liquids, slowly, over a spoon, in the order below.

The reason this experiment works is because liquids with different densities don't mix.

| 1 | 2 | 3 | 4 | 5 |

Honey

Milk

Washing-up liquid

Water
with added
food colouring

Oil

Sink or swim?

Drop objects into the mix and see if they sink or float. The objects will float on whichever liquid has a lower density than they do.

An object or substance's density is how much matter is packed into the space it takes up.

Oil

Water

Washing-up liquid

Milk

Honey

The ping pong ball is filled with air so has a low density.

Blue soda water

Cranberry juice

Orange juice

Here's a second density experiment that you can drink!

Fizzing **balloon**

Impress your friends with this amazing science experiment that causes a chemical reaction you can see with your own eyes.

You will need:
- bottle
- funnel
- vinegar
- food colouring (optional)
- 2 tbsp baking soda
- balloon

1 Fill 1/3 of the bottle with vinegar and add a drop of food colouring.

2 Clean the funnel and use it to put the baking soda into the balloon.

3 Place the neck of the balloon over the bottle, being careful not to let any baking soda drop inside.

4 Lift the balloon up so the baking soda drops into the bottle. Now watch the chemical reaction!

Gas

How it works

When the baking soda and vinegar mix, it causes a chemical reaction. This reaction produces a gas called **carbon dioxide** that blows up the balloon!

As the gas rises up out of the bottle, it is trapped by the balloon. This causes the balloon to inflate.

The baking soda is a solid, the vinegar is a liquid, and the carbon dioxide is a gas. These are all different "states of matter".

Liquid

Templates

These templates will come in handy when making two of the trickier projects in the book. Carefully copy them onto card and you can use them multiple times.

Jetpack (pages 20-21)

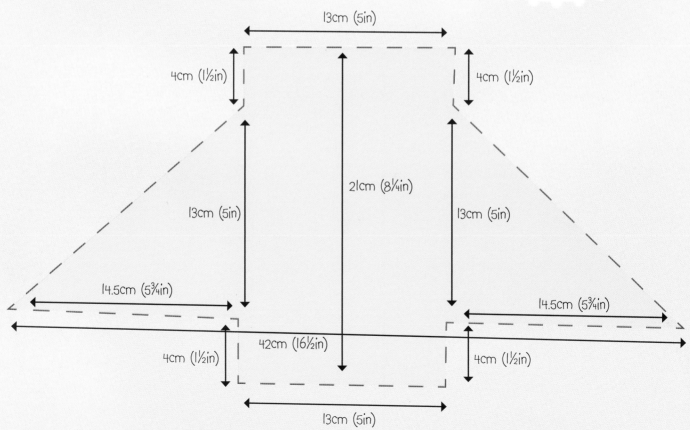

13cm (5in)

4cm (1½in)

4cm (1½in)

21cm (8¼in)

13cm (5in)

13cm (5in)

14.5cm (5¾in)

14.5cm (5¾in)

42cm (16½in)

4cm (1½in)

4cm (1½in)

13cm (5in)

Pyramid money box (page 44-45)

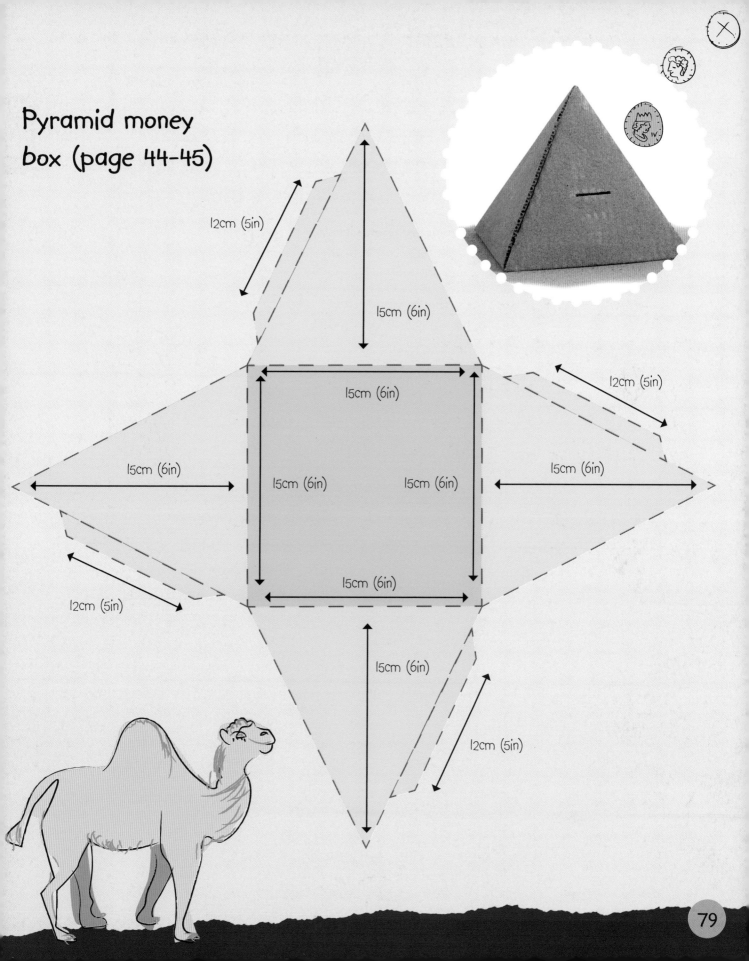

12cm (5in)

15cm (6in)

15cm (6in)

15cm (6in)

15cm (6in)

15cm (6in)

12cm (5in)

15cm (6in)

12cm (5in)

15cm (6in)

15cm (6in)

12cm (5in)

Index

Acknowledgements

The publisher would like to thank the following for their kind permission to reproduce their photographs:
(Key: a-above; b-below/bottom; c-centre; f-far; l-left; r-right; t-top)

3 Alamy Stock Photo: Brian Hagiwara / Brand X Pictures (crb/beetle). 4 Dreamstime.com: Koolander (tr). 6 Dreamstime.com: Torian Dixon / Mrincredible (crb/Earth). 7 Dreamstime.com: Torian Dixon / Mrincredible (tr/Uranus & Neptune). 14 Dreamstime.com: Koolander (clb); Konstantin Shaklein / 3dsculptor (main rocket). 15 123RF.com: Boris Stromar / astrobobo (br). Dreamstime.com: Eddie Toro (c). 18 Dorling Kindersley: Dave Shayler / Astro Info Service Ltd (clb/all badges, except Apollo 7). 23 Science Photo Library: NASA Earth Observatory (br). 24-25 iStockphoto.com: FrankvandenBergh (tree in 4 seasons). 24 Dreamstime.com: Jens Stolt / Jpsdk (tr). 25 Dreamstime.com: Ralf Neumann / Ingwio (tc); Geert Weggen / Geertweggen (bc). 32 iStockphoto.com: AlinaMD (cr); FamVeld (cl). 33 123RF.com: alphaspirit (bl, br); Rune Kristoffersen / rknis (cr). iStockphoto.com: Smitt (cl). 40-41 iStockphoto.com: Holger Mette / holgs (pyramid). 45 iStockphoto.com: Holger Mette / holgs (cra). 47 Dorling Kindersley: Newcastle Great Northern Museum, Hancock, (bl). 48 Alamy Stock Photo: David Stares (clb). 48-49 123RF.com: freeartist (cb). Alamy Stock Photo: Lebrecht Music and Arts Photo Library (map background). 49 123RF.com: glevalex (cla). Alamy Stock Photo: Elizabeth Hak (br); INTERFOTO (cla/Tiberius coin). 51 Alamy Stock Photo: David Stares (bl). 52 Dreamstime.com: Chris Hill / Ca2hill (bl). 53 Dreamstime.com: Chris Hill / Ca2hill (cl/coins). 56 Alamy Stock Photo: Brian Hagiwara / Brand X Pictures (cl). Dorling Kindersley: Forrest L. Mitchell / James Laswel (cla). Dreamstime.com: Stu Porter / Stuporter (cr). 57 123RF.com: Andrejs Pidjass / NejroN (cra). Dreamstime.com: Dirk Ercken / Kikkerdirk (bl/frog). 68 123RF.com: Oleksandr Marynchenko (crb/light bulb). 68-69 Dreamstime.com: Supertrooper (b/grass).

All other images © Dorling Kindersley
For further information see: www.dkimages.com

DK would like to thank:

Myriam Megharbi for picture library assistance, Violet Peto for proofreading, and Julie Stewart for photography assistance.